WHAT ARE MASTERPIECES

WHAT ARE MASTERPIECES

PITMAN PUBLISHING CORPORATION

By GERTRUDE STEIN

NEW YORK   TORONTO   LONDON   TEL AVIV

CONTENTS

The drawings of Gertrude Stein and of Basket are by Francis Picabia

ANOTHER GARLAND FOR GERTRUDE STEIN

WHILE Gertrude Stein was a student at Radcliffe she took a course she liked immensely. She likes lots of things immensely, but this she did like more than others. It was a course in cloud-formation, she wrote to me about it just the other day. And the other day, quite by accident, I learned from a fellow-Californian that the Bay-region around San Francisco is one of the finest in the world for the observation of cloud phenomena. Now Stein says that at Bilignin too (in the Rhone River valley where she spends her summers) the sky is the bluest and the clouds are the nicest of any!

But Gertrude Stein is a Californian—that is, we Californians appropriate her as such. Although she was actually born in Allegheny, Pennsylvania, she spent most of her youth under the clouds of Oakland and San Francisco. In *The Making of Americans* she has written of them, these clouds of California, as "the firm white summer clouds breaking away from the horizon and slowly moving." I like to think that they helped to make her what she is more than the other clouds of America she has lived under—certainly more than the clouds of Belley or Paris which have, it is true, been over her while she has lived out the last three decades of her writing.

And possibly this is so, for throughout her writing (as in the second lecture of this book) she has insisted, "I am an American and I have lived half my life in Paris, not the half which made me but the half in which I made what I made." Perhaps the "breaking away and slowly moving" American clouds did help her first to see and then to say what is in "Composition as Explanation," just as Paris has helped her to what she says in "An American and France." I hope it is true, but you may judge for yourself. It is a grave matter, believe me—a matter of pride if you are an ardent Californian who wants the poetry of Gertrude Stein as well as the clouds of California to belong to you.

II

Possibly the most adequate account of Gertrude Stein's early accomplishments is to be found printed on the dust-jacket of her book *Geography and Plays*. It reads: "Gertrude Stein was born in Allegheny, Pennsylvania, but her early years were spent in Vienna and Paris. From Europe she was taken to California and there educated in public schools until she was seventeen. At Radcliffe College she became interested in Psychology and Philosophy and worked under Münsterberg and William James, who both predicted a remarkable future for her. While at Radcliffe she published her psychological experiments. Under the stimulation of this subject she decided to study medicine and from Radcliffe entered the Johns Hopkins Medical School. Practical Medicine did not particularly interest her and soon she specialized in the anatomy of the brain and the direction of brain tracts.

"But insistently Gertrude Stein was an artist and towards the end of her last year at Johns Hopkins she dismayed her friends with the statement that she was not going to be a scientist and then went for a year to England. She stayed one more year in America and then went to live in Paris, which is her present home. Here she wrote and published her first book, *Three Lives*. She at once came into contact with the young school of painters. She found Picasso, and her close, friendly association with him is common knowledge. She wrote a long book called *The Making of Americans Being the History of a Family's Progress*, which she used as a study of style. Out of this book has sprung what is called the modern school of writing. She published short things, portraits of those who frequented her home—Matisse and Picasso, now so well known among her friends, among the number—and the two famous books, *The Portrait of Mabel Dodge* and *Tender Buttons.*

"Then came the war, and Gertrude Stein drove a Ford car called Auntie, and visited hospitals, and was decorated by the French government with the medal of the Reconnaissance Française. She ended up her work entering Alsace with the French Army."

In the course of the eight years which followed the war, Gertrude Stein created constantly. Even while publishers were frankly indifferent to her, she went on growing—by expressing the growth of the epoch in which she lived. There was a steadily increasing public interest, however, in that part of her work which from time to time did get into print. Fugitive pieces printed in magazines both here and abroad were slowly creating for her a place in American letters. Carl Van Vechten, writing in the preface to *Four Saints in Three Acts,* has said, "It is doubtless true that any worthy work of art seldom languishes long unheard in this world of ours." Accordingly, it was not long after the war before publishers turned at last to Gertrude Stein. Two substantial volumes of her work were published: in America in 1922, *Geography and Plays;* in Paris in 1925, *The Making of Americans* in its complete form. Then, as a climax to the first two decades of writing, came the invitations from the Oxford and Cambridge literary societies requesting that Gertrude Stein address them in 1926.

Following this address, for which Gertrude Stein wrote *Composition as Explanation,* began the series of rapid printings which have since made nearly all of her major works available. Almost immediately, Leonard and Virginia Woolfe printed the lecture in their Hogarth Essay Series. The American edition, by Doubleday-Doran, was printed in 1927. In 1927, Galerie Simon did as *As a Wife Has a Cow a Love Story,* and went on the following year with the play *A Village*. In America, also in 1928, Payson-Clarke, Ltd. produced *Useful Knowledge*. In 1929, the Seizin Press of London undertook *An Acquaintance with Description*. In 1930, the novel *Lucy Church Amiably* appeared. In 1931, Plain Edition printed the meditations on grammar, *How to Write*, as well as the poems *Before the Flowers of Friendship Faded Friendship Faded*. In 1932, Plain Edition went on with *Operas and Plays* and the important *Long Gay Book*. By this time Stein had become recognizably a literary celebrity, especially in her own America, where, since 1932, the printing of her books has principally gone on. In 1933, for example, Modern Library reprinted *Three Lives* in a popular edition. The Atlantic Monthly, Harcourt-Brace, and later the Literary Guild published and made a best-seller of *The Autobiography of Alice B. Toklas*. In 1934, Harcourt-Brace did a popular edition of *The Making of Americans*. In the same year Random House printed the volume *Portraits and Prayers*, and the libretto of *Four Saints in Three Acts*, which was appearing on Broadway. Following Stein's brilliant lecture tour of America in 1935, came the volume *Lectures in America*. During the tour, and at the invitation of the University of Chicago, Stein wrote and delivered the lectures subsequently printed by the University Press as *Narration*. Random House, in 1936, published *The Geographical History of America or The Relation of Human Nature to the Human Mind*. In the next year, done by the same publisher, appeared the volume which records the experiences of the American tour: *Everybody's Autobiography*. In 1938, the *Picasso* appeared in three countries. In 1939, Gertrude Stein's first book for children, *The World is Round*, was printed—in America by William R. Scott, with illustrations by Clemence

Hurd—in England by Batsford, with illustrations by Sir Francis Rose. This year news comes of an Italian translation of *Three Lives*, by Einaudi of Turin, and of the new book, *Paris France*, published by Batsford of London and Scribners of New York.

In any kind of proportion, as Stein might say, this is a lot of printing for one decade of any author's life!

In terms of printed works, then, Stein had become a "successful" author; in terms of writers, finally, Stein had become the Dr. Johnson of American letters; in terms of readers, more importantly, she had become (through the sheer exercise of that delicate wit embodied in the book she chose to call *The Autobiography of Alice B. Toklas*) something that the weighty English Samuel had never the honesty nor the humor to become for himself—her own Boswell!

III

In 1926, then, Stein delivered before the students of Oxford and Cambridge Universities her first remarkable lecture, "Composition as Explanation." Readers of the first *Autobiography* well know the story of that memorable excursion to England. Doubtless they also remember Stein's description of the chilly mechanic's shed in Montrouge where she wrote the whole of the lecture while she watched her old Ford dismantled and repaired.

To the audience that first heard it, "Composition as Explanation" may have seemed to contain the ideas of a literary iconoclast. As we Americans now read it, however, we recognize in the undercurrent of its ideas important facets in the cultural temper of our Twentieth Century. It soon becomes evident that here is no mere exposition of Stein's literary methods; here, rather, is a vital and uncompromising commentary upon the change in categories wrought within that Mind which has grown naturally to conceive and accept the Pragmatic attitude.

Pragmatists will tell you that time and change and chance are the realities of the universe; that all knowledge (whether of the present or of the past) is presently held, and that this present is in continual flux. Stein, seeking perhaps to express the reality of change (in which substantive and transitive elements appear as con-substantial) says in "Composition as Explanation," "Everything being alike everything naturally everything is different simply different naturally simply different."

Horace M. Kallen, in his introduction to the Modern Library edition of *The Philosophy of William James*, has described the character of James' changing world in this way: "Suppose you take the world as it comes. Suppose you take the world at its face value. Then reality is what you know it as. You find the substantive parts of it connected by relations as truly present and existent as the parts themselves. You find transition and change, continuity and discontinuity, routine and surprises, multiple unities of manifold kinds, realities of various stuffs and powers, all connected with one another by transitions from next to next, and each standing away, alone, unmitigated, unincludable, now from some things, now from others. You find movement. You find beginnings, you find endings. You find continuity and you find transformation. In a word, the world of the daily life which we touch and see and hear and smell and taste, which we struggle against and work together with, need be none other than we experience it to be . . .

"In sum, thus, James is a metaphysical democrat. His philosophy admits everything that can be named to establish its status in the stream of place we call the universe. There, in all-generating and none-favoring nature, no one thing has greater right or more virtue than any other. Every item is tentative, adventurous, experimental, unfinished; nothing is; each thing becomes; change and growth are in each. So in fleeing the genteel tradition, James found America."[1]

This is the world of flux and presentness which Stein brings to the attention in "Composition as Explanation." "Composition," to interpret the terminology, is "what is seen." It is the composition, Stein says, "and the time of and the time in the composition" which changes. In this seen world no one thing changes—for all things are change.

In her early writing, Stein sought to register the reality of this change by "beginning again and again and again," by keeping "simply different as an intention," and by "groping for a continuous present." Later, when she had "mastered very much" what she was doing, she was not, she tells us, so deliberate in her intention. "Whether there was or whether there was not a continuous present did not then any longer trouble me . . . there was or there was . . ."

It becomes very clear, in a world in which no thing may be said to change because everything is change, why there was no need to keep "simply different as an intention." Change was inevitable, "the whole of it was inevitable."

The words, "a composition of a prolonged present is a natural composition in the world as it has been these last thirty years," leave little doubt, furthermore, as to what Stein has

[1]H. M. Kallen, *The Philosophy of William James*. Modern Library.

considered to be the characterizing point of view of her generation. It is the attitude of Pragmatism, with its conception of the world as an ongoing present event, and with its consequent categories of changing process, texture, strands, environment, spread, quality, fusion, blocking and novelty. It is this philosophical attitude which finds ultimate reality in that aspect of the world which it describes as continuous. It is this same continuity which Gertrude Stein has alluded to as the "prolonged present."

Perhaps a systematic study of Gertrude Stein's aesthetics would best begin here, for the ongoing present event (which might be called the root-metaphor of the pragmatic philosophy) is a conception which permeates her writing.

"The business of Art," she says, "is to live in the actual present, that is the complete actual present, and to express that complete actual present."[2] This is, in effect, Gertrude Stein's definition of her aesthetic field; the unmistakable definition of a pragmatic thinker. When this is realized, perhaps we will at last admit that we are dealing with a truly philosophical poet.

But to explore for a moment the further implications of "Composition as Explanation." How are we to understand "the time of" and "the time in" the composition?

The "composition" has been defined as "what is seen;" what is seen depends upon the way "everybody is doing everything." The two indispensible elements in this analysis are a seer or perceiver of the composition, and the seen or creators of the composition. Besides this, we know that the time of

[2]Gertrude Stein, *Lectures in America*. Random House, 1935. Pp. 104-5.

and the time in the composition are in flux—ever different.

The time of the composition might be taken to denote the chronologically located time-span during which a perceiver regards "the way everybody is doing everything." The time in the composition, on the other hand, would denote the pattern of activities characterizing this span at any given time. For example: The making of motor-trucks is an activity thus far peculiar to the Twentieth Century. Thus the making of motor-trucks forms a portion of the composition of the century. The time of that portion of the composition is the Twentieth Century. The time in that portion of the composition is the unique pattern of activities (the series of techniques and devices) relevant to the mass production of motor-trucks. Each century and each portion of a century evolves its own methods for doing something in particular. This gives each its particular tempo. The recognition of composition comes when the uniqueness of these activities is realized by a perceiver.

In sum, one might say that the epoch which conditions the life of the artist also conditions the character of the art which he makes. "The composition is the thing seen by everyone living in the living they are doing, they are the composing of the composition that at the time they are living is the composition of the time in which they are living. It is that that makes living a thing they are doing." It is that, too, which "makes what those who describe it make of it," for the composition which the artist makes as his art is dependent upon the composition which he sees as his life. It is dependent upon his moment of seeing; it is dependent upon his recognition of the particular character of the composition in which he lives his life.

It is this unique complex or composition which is seen by

those "who are creating the modern composition authentically" in the arts. The realization of this uniqueness, and its inevitable relationship to the artist's own way of "doing everything," in turn qualifies the character of his creative work and makes it "compose as it does."

Thornton Wilder has reported Stein to say that "the artist is the most sensitive exponent of his contemporaneousness, expressing it while it still lies in the unconscious of society at large."[3] As an artist of the present, it is his business to express the particular composition of that actual present in which he lives, and to embody it sensitively and authentically and presently in a created composition of "complete actual present."

This, in one way, is the explanation by composition.

When Stein speaks in "Composition as Explanation" of a "continuous present a beginning again and again" and of "including more and more using of everything," she is enunciating in her own manner the very standards relevant to the work of art which takes as its business the expression of the "complete actual present." Pragmatic aesthetics defines beauty as existing in proportion to the quality of present events. In the words of Professor Stephen Pepper, for example, "the most beautiful given event is that which is the most vivid in quality and the most extensive in texture." The aesthetic field, for the pragmatist, is "that of the quality of events—for in the end, nothing is valuable but the quality of something."[4]

Why do present events become the particular business of art? Because for the pragmatic thinker only immediate ex-

[3]Thornton Wilder, Preface to *Narration* by Gertrude Stein. University of Chicago Press, 1935.
[4]Stephen Pepper, *Aesthetic Quality*. Scribners, 1937.

perience is vivid and real. "And if," writes Pepper, "the quality is extensive, rich and vivid, it is beauty in the high sense of the term."[5]

Consequently, in the later lecture, "What are Masterpieces," the aesthetic implications of this psychological fact are further formulated. Stein discredits all remembered experience as slack and unsubstantial. Applying this to the problems of creation, she says: "If you continue to remember your writing gets very confused." Hence expository writing, which is all memory writing, she pronounces "lifeless" and "so dull."

For memory, so to speak, employs two times: the time remembered and the time of remembering. When there are these two times, the present self becomes audience to its own past. "I am I because my little dog knows me," illustrates such an employment of memory; it results in the confusion Stein terms "identity." When there is but one time, on the other hand, there is "entity"; it results in the creation of masterpieces. The "I am I yes sir I am I" of the puppet play illustrates this denial of memory in favor of the expression of what is immediately or actually present. For the creation of an art, the goal of which is the expression of the "complete actual present," it is clear that there must be but one time, and that the present time.

IV

How far Stein has deliberately subscribed to the philosophic attitude which has here been suggested, may best be determined by those who know and study the gradual evolution of her work. After an examination of the course of her development, I myself think that the changes in literary method

[5]Ibid.

which are apparent in it are significant in that they progressively contributed to the frank espousal of the aesthetics consistent with such a philosophical attitude. It is little surprising that the ideas of William James have influenced his pupil. It is remarkable, however, to realize that Stein has, from her first work forward, created in an aesthetics which did not have its formal doctrination until as late as two decades after her first experiments with it. It is to be understood literally that the rudiments of a pragmatic aesthetic appeared in her work before contemporary philosophers, including William James, had expounded such an aesthetic. It was, then, with the voice of annunciation that she said, in 1926, "naturally no one thinks, that is no one formulates until what is to be formulated has been made."

The whole of her creative writing seems to be the natural expression of this aesthetics in works of art. This present collection is, however, the record of the formulation in her works of criticism.

If William James, as Ralph Barton Perry would have it, "was left to develop an indigenous American philosophy, the first, perhaps, in which the American experience escaped the stamp of an imported ideology," students of Gertrude Stein would assert that it was left to her to go beyond James and to develop an indigenous American aesthetics, the first, perhaps, in which the American aesthetic experience has escaped the stamp of an imported ideology.

Who else has for over thirty years struggled to give our literature the backbone of a native metaphysic? Were Stein only a literary thinker, the singular contribution of these lectures to the history of aesthetics would more than secure her fame on the "long road of American letters." But to recognize that aspect of her work alone is to overlook the three decades of steady literary creation to which she has besides devoted herself.

Examples of that creation are also contained in this volume. When Stein delivered "Composition as Explanation" in 1926, she appended to her reading the four examples from her own work exactly as they are reprinted in this volume; a poem, two portraits, and a play. The puppet play, written ten years later, was placed between the later lectures as an excellent example of her recent development, since it derives from *The Geographical History of America* or *The Relation of Human Nature to the Human Mind*.

One point further, lest there be any misunderstanding. It has hardly been my intention to suggest that the purpose of Gertrude Stein's creative writing has been merely the exposition of a particular philosophical system. On the contrary; here we are facing the spontaneous creation of vivid and concentrated literary pieces which show her constantly to have been placing literature on a plane superior to philosophy and science. They are not philosophy; they are not science. But science and philosophy, often, are what they talk about. For science and philosophy make up, in our time, important strands of the composition in which we live.

It is my hope, therefore, that this volume will redirect the attention of readers to Gertrude Stein's purely creative writings. The few suggestions in this preface concerning the philosophical foundations of her criticism are likewise only very humbly intended to suggest to students a new approach to the enjoyment of her work.

ROBERT BARTLETT HAAS
September, 1940

COMPOSITION AS EXPLANATION

COMPOSITION AS EXPLANATION

THERE is singularly nothing that makes a difference a difference in beginning and in the middle and in ending except that each generation has something different at which they are all looking. By this I mean so simply that anybody knows it that composition is the difference which makes each and all of them then different from other generations and this is what makes everything different otherwise they are all alike and everybody knows it because everybody says it.

It is very likely that nearly every one has been very nearly certain that something that is interesting is interesting them. Can they and do they. It is very interesting that nothing inside in them, that is when you consider the very long history of how every one ever acted or has felt, it is very interesting that nothing inside in them in all of them makes it connectedly different. By this I mean this. The only thing that is different from one time to another is what is seen and what is seen depends upon how everybody is doing everything. This makes the thing we are looking at very different and this makes what those describe it make of it, it makes a composition, it confuses, it shows, it is, it looks, it likes it as it is, and this makes what is seen as it is seen. Nothing changes from generation to generation except the thing seen and that makes a composition. Lord Grey remarked that when the generals before the war talked about the war they talked about it as a nineteenth-century war although to be fought with twentieth-century weapons. That is because war is a thing that decides how it is to be done when it is to be done. It is prepared and to that degree it is like all academies it is not a thing made by being made it is a thing prepared. Writing and painting and all that, is like that, for those who occupy themselves with it and don't make it as it is made. Now the few who make it as it is made, and it is to be remarked that the most decided of them usually are prepared just as the world around them is preparing, do it in this way and so I if you do not mind I will tell you how it happens. Naturally one does not know how it happened until it is well over beginning happening.

To come back to the part that the only thing that is different is what is seen when it seems to be being seen, in other words, composition and time sense.

No one is ahead of his time, it is only that the particular variety of creating his time is the one that his contemporaries who also are creating their own time refuse to accept. And they refuse to accept it for a very simple reason and that is that they do not have to accept it for any reason. They themselves that is everybody in their entering the modern composition and they do enter it, if they do not enter it they are not so to speak in it they are out of it and so they do enter it; but in as you may say the non-competitive efforts where if you are not in it nothing is lost except nothing at all except what is not had, there are naturally all the refusals, and the things refused are only important if unexpectedly somebody happens to need them. In the case of the arts it is very definite. Those who are creating the modern composition authentically are naturally only of importance when they are dead because by that time the modern composition having become past is classified and the description of it is classical. That is the reason why the creator of the new composition in the arts is an outlaw until he is a classic, there is hardly a moment in between and it is really too bad very much too bad naturally for the creator but also very much too bad for the enjoyer, they all really would enjoy the created so much better just after it has been made than when it is already a classic, but it is perfectly simple that there is no reason why

27

the contemporary should see, because it would not make any difference as they lead their lives in the new composition anyway, and as every one is naturally indolent why naturally they don't see. For this reason as in quoting Lord Grey it is quite certain that nations not actively threatened are at least several generations behind themselves militarily so aesthetically they are more than several generations behind themselves and it is very much too bad, it is so very much more exciting and satisfactory for everybody if one can have contemporaries, if all one's contemporaries could be one's contemporaries.

There is almost not an interval.

For a very long time everybody refuses and then almost without a pause almost everybody accepts. In the history of the refused in the arts and literature the rapidity of the change is always startling. Not the only difficulty with the *volte-face* concerning the arts is this. When the acceptance comes, by that acceptance the thing created becomes a classic. It is a natural phenomena a rather extraordinary natural phenomena that a thing accepted becomes a classic. And what is the characteristic quality of a classic. The characteristic quality of a classic is that it is beautiful. Now of course it is perfectly true that a more or less first rate work of art is beautiful but the trouble is that when that first rate work of art becomes a classic because it is accepted the only thing that is important from then on to the majority of the acceptors the enormous majority, the most intelligent majority of the acceptors is that it is so wonderfully beautiful. Of course it is wonderfully beautiful, only when it is still a thing irritating annoying stimulating then all quality of beauty is denied to it.

Of course it is beautiful but first all beauty in it is denied and then all the beauty of it is accepted. If every one were not so indolent they would realize that beauty is beauty even when it is irritating and stimulating not only when it is accepted and classic. Of course it is extremely difficult nothing more so than to remember back to its not being beautiful once it has become beautiful. This makes it so much more difficult to realize its beauty when the work is being refused and prevents every one from realizing that they were convinced that beauty was denied, once the work is accepted. Automatically with the acceptance of the time sense comes the recognition of the beauty and once the beauty is accepted the beauty never fails any one.

Beginning again and again is a natural thing even when there is a series.

Beginning again and again and again explaining composition and time is a natural thing.

It is understood by this time that everything is the same except composition and time, composition and the time of the composition and the time in the composition.

Everything is the same except composition and as the composition is different and always going to be different everything is not the same. Everything is not the same as the time when of the composition and the time in the composition is different. The composition is different, that is certain.

The composition is the thing seen by every one living in the living that they are doing, they are the composing of the composition that at the time they are living is the composition of the time in which they are living. It is that that makes living a thing they are doing. Nothing else is different, of that almost any one can be certain. The time when and the time of and the time in that composition is the natural phenomena of that composition and of that perhaps every one can be certain.

No one thinks these things when they are making when they are creating what is the composition, naturally no one thinks, that is no one formulates until what is to be formulated has been made.

Composition is not there, it is going to be there and we are here. This is some time ago for us naturally.

The only thing that is different from one time to another is what is seen and what is seen depends upon how everybody is doing everything. This makes the thing we are looking at very different and this makes what those who describe it make of it, it makes a composition, it confuses, it shows, it is, it looks, it likes it as it is, and this makes what is seen as it is seen. Nothing changes from generation to generation except the thing seen and that makes a composition.

Now the few who make writing as it is made and it is to be remarked that the most decided of them are those that are prepared by preparing, are prepared just as the world around them is prepared and is preparing to do it in this way and so if you do not mind I will again tell you how it hapens. Naturally one does not know how it happened until it is well over beginning happening.

Each period of living differs from any other period of living not in the way life is but in the way life is conducted and that authentically speaking is composition. After life has been conducted in a certain way everybody knows it but nobody knows it, little by little, nobody knows it as long as nobody knows it. Any one creating the composition in the arts does not know it either, they are conducting life and that makes their composition what it is, it makes their work compose as it does.

Their influence and their influences are the same as that of all of their contemporaries only it must always be remembered that the analogy is not obvious until as I say the composition of a time has become so pronounced that it is past and the artistic composition of it is a classic.

And now to begin as if to begin. Composition is not there, it is going to be there and we are here. This is some time ago for us naturally. There is something to be added afterwards.

Just how much my work is known to you I do not know. I feel that perhaps it would be just as well to tell the whole of it.

In beginning writing I wrote a book called *Three Lives* this was written in 1905. I wrote a negro story called *Melanctha*. In that there was a constant recurring and beginning there was a marked direction in the direction of being in the present although naturally I had been accustomed to past present and future, and why, because the composition forming around me was a prolonged present. A composition of a prolonged present is a natural composition in the world as it has been these thirty years it was more and more a prolonged present. I created then a prolonged present naturally I knew nothing of a continuous present but it came naturally to me to make one, it was simple it was clear to me and nobody knew why it was done like that, I did not myself although naturally to me it was natural.

After that I did a book called *The Making of Americans* it is a long book about a thousand pages.

Here again it was all so natural to me and more and more complicatedly a continuous present. A continuous present is a continuous present. I made almost a thousand pages of a continuous present.

Continuous present is one thing and beginning again and

again is another thing. These are both things. And then there is using everything.

This brings us again to composition this the using every-thing. The using everything brings us to composition and to this composition. A continuous present and using everything and beginning again. In these two books there was elaboration of the complexities of using everything and of a continuous present and of beginning again and again and again.

In the first book there was a groping for a continuous present and for using everything by beginning again and again.

There was a groping for using everything and there was a groping for a continuous present and there was an inevitable beginning of beginning again and again and again.

Having naturally done this I naturally was a little troubled with it when I read it. I became then like the others who read it. One does, you know, excepting that when I reread it myself I lost myself in it again. Then I said to myself this time it will be different and I began. I did not begin again I just began.

In this beginning naturally since I at once went on and on very soon there were pages and pages and pages more and more elaborated creating a more and more continuous present including more and more using of everything and continuing more and more beginning and beginning and beginning.

I went on and on to a thousand pages of it.

In the meantime to naturally begin I commenced making portraits of anybody and anything. In making these portraits I naturally made a continuous present an including every-thing and a beginning again and again within a very small thing. That started me into composing anything into one thing. So then naturally it was natural that one thing an enormously long thing was not everything an enormously short thing was also not everything nor was it all of it a continuous present thing nor was it always and always beginning again. Naturally I would then begin again. I would begin again I would naturally begin. I did naturally begin. This brings me to a great deal that has been begun.

And after that what changes what changes after that, after that what changes and what changes after that and after that and what changes and after that and what changes after that.

The problem from this time on became more definite.

It was all so nearly alike it must be different and it is different, it is natural that if everything is used and there is a continuous present and a beginning again and again if it is all so alike it must be simply different and everything simply different was the natural way of creating it then.

In this natural way of creating it then that it was simply different everything being alike it was simply different, this kept on leading one to lists. Lists naturally for a while and by lists I mean a series. More and more in going back over what was done at this time I find that I naturally kept simply different as an intention. Whether there was or whether there was not a continuous present did not then any longer trouble me there was or there was, and using everything no longer troubled me if everything is alike using everything could no longer trouble me and beginning again and again could no longer trouble me because if lists were inevitable if series were inevitable and the whole of it was inevitable beginning again and again could not trouble me so then with nothing to trouble me I very completely began naturally since everything is alike making it as simply different naturally as simply different as possible. I began doing natural phenomena what I call natural phenomena and natural phenomena naturally everything being alike natural phenomena are making things be naturally simply different. This found its culmination later, in the beginning it began in a center confused with lists with series with geography with returning portraits and with particularly often four and three and often with five and four. It is easy to see that in the beginning such a conception as everything being naturally different would be very inarticulate and very slowly it began to emerge and take the form of anything, and then naturally if anything that is simply different is simply different what follows will follow.

So far then the progress of my conceptions was the natural progress entirely in accordance with my epoch as I am sure is to be quite easily realized if you think over the scene that was before us all from year to year.

As I said in the beginning, there is the long history of how every one ever acted or has felt and that nothing inside in them in all of them makes it connectedly different. By this I mean all this.

The only thing that is different from one time to another is what is seen and what is seen depends upon how everybody is doing everything.

It is understood by this time that everything is the same except composition and time, composition and the time of the composition and the time in the composition.

Everything is the same except composition and as the composition is different and always going to be different everything is not the same. So then I as a contemporary creating the composition in the beginning was groping toward a continuous present, a using everything a beginning again and again and then everything being alike then everything very simply everything was naturally simply different and so I as a contemporary was creating everything being alike was creating everything naturally being naturally simply different, everything being alike. This then was the period that brings me to the period of the beginning of 1914. Everything being alike everything naturally would be simply different and war came and everything being alike and everything being simply different brings everything being simply different brings it to romanticism.

Romanticism is then when everything being alike everything is naturally simply different, and romanticism.

Then for four years this was more and more different even though this was, was everything alike. Everything alike naturally everything was simply different and this is and was romanticism and this is and was war. Everything being alike everything naturally everything is different simply different naturally simply different.

And so there was the natural phenomena that was war, which had been, before war came, several generations behind the contemporary composition, because it became war and so completely needed to be contemporary became completely contemporary and so created the completed recognition of the contemporary composition. Every one but one may say every one became consciously became aware of the existence of the authenticity of the modern composition. This then the contemporary recognition, because of the academic thing known as war having been forced to become contemporary made every one not only contemporary in act not only contemporary in thought but contemporary in self-consciousness made every one contemporary with the modern composition. And so the art creation of the contemporary composition which would have been outlawed normally outlawed several genera-

35

tions more behind even than war, war having been brought so to speak up to date art so to speak was allowed not completely to be up to date, but nearly up to date, in other words we who created the expression of the modern composition were to be recognized before we were dead some of us even quite a long time before we were dead. And so war may be said to have advanced a general recognition of the expression of the contemporary composition by almost thirty years.

And now after that there is no more of that in other words there is peace and something comes then and it follows coming then.

And so now one finds oneself interesting oneself in an equilibration, that of course means words as well as things and distribution as well as between themselves between the words and themselves and the things and themselves, a distribution as distributuion. This makes what follows what follows and now there is every reason why there should be an arrangement made. Distribution is interesting and equilibration is interesting when a continuous present and a beginning again and again and using everything and everything alike and everything naturally simply different has been done.

After all this, there is that, there has been that that there is a composition and that nothing changes except composition the composition and the time of and the time in the composition.

The time of the composition is a natural thing and the time in the composition is a natural thing it is a natural thing and it is a contemporary thing.

The time of the composition is the time of the composition. It has been at times a present thing it has been at times a past thing it has been at times a future thing it has been at times an endeavour at parts or all of these things. In my beginning it was a continuous present a beginning again and again and again and again, it was a series it was a list it was a similarity and everything different it was a distribution and an equilibration. That is all of the time some of the time of the composition.

Now there is still something else the time-sense in the composition. This is what is always a fear a doubt and a judgement and a conviction. The quality in the creation of expression the quality in a composition that makes it go dead just after it has been made is very troublesome.

The time in the composition is a thing that is very troublesome. If the time in the composition is very troublesome it is because there must even if there is no time at all in the composition there must be time in the composition which is in its quality of distribution and equilibration. In the beginning there was the time in the composition that naturally was in the composition but time in the composition comes now and this is what is now troubling every one the time in the composition is now a part of distribution and equilibration. In the beginning there was confusion there was a continuous present and later there was romanticism which was not a confusion but an extrication and now there is either succeeding or failing there must be distribution and equilibration there must be time that is distributed and equilibrated. This is the thing that is at present the most troubling and if there is the time that is at present the most troublesome the time-sense that is at present the most troubling is the thing that makes the present the most troubling. There is at present there is distribution, by this I mean expression and time, and in this way at present composition is time that is the reason that at present the time-sense is troubling that is the reason why at present the time-sense in the composition is the composition that is making what there is in composition.

And afterwards.

Now that is all.

1926

PRECIOSILLA

C<small>OUSIN TO</small> C<small>LARE</small> W<small>ASHING</small>.
I<small>N</small> the win all the band beagles which have cousin lime sign
and arrange a weeding match to presume a certain point to

exstate to exstate a certain pass lint to exstate a lean sap prime lo and shut shut is life.

Bait, bait tore, tore her clothes, toward it, toward a bit, to ward a sit, sit down in, in vacant surely lots, a single mingle, bait and wet, wet a single establishment that has a lily lily grow. Come to the pen come in the stem, come in the grass grown water.

Lily wet lily wet while. This is so pink so pink in stammer, a long bean which shows bows is collected by a single curly shady, shady get, get set wet bet.

It is a snuff a snuff to be told and have can witer, can is it and sleep sleeps knot, it is a lily scarf the pink and blue yellow, not blue not odour sun, nobles are bleeding bleeding two seats two seats on end. Why is grief. Grief is strange black. Sugar is melting. We will not swim.

PRECIOSILLA

Please be please be get, please get wet, wet naturally, naturally in weather. Could it be fire more firier. Could it be so in ate struck. Could it be gold up, gold up stringing, in it while while which is hanging, hanging in dingling, dingling in pinning, not so. Not so dots large dressed dots, big sizes, less laced, less laced diamonds, diamonds white, diamonds bright, diamonds in the in the light, diamonds light diamonds door diamonds hanging to be four, two four, all before, this bean, lessly, all most, a best, willow, vest, a green guest, guest, go go go go go go go. Go go. Not guessed. Go go.

Toasted susie is my ice-cream.

A SAINT IN SEVEN

I THOUGHT perhaps that we would win by human means, I
knew we could win if we did win but I did not think that we

could win by human means, and now we have won by human means.

A saint followed and not surrounded.

LIST OF PERSONAGES

1. A saint with a lily.

Second. A girl with a rooster in front of her and a bush of strange flowers at her side and a small tree behind her.

3. A guardian of a museum holding a cane.

4. A woman leaning forward.

5. A woman with a sheep in front of her a small tree behind her.

6. A woman with black hair and two bundles one under each arm.

7. A night watchman of a hotel who does not fail to stand all the time.

8. A very stout girl with a basket and flowers summer flowers and the flowers are in front of a small tree.

SAINTS IN SEASON

See Saints in seven.

And how do royalists accuse themselves.

Saints.

Saint Joseph.

In pleading sadness length of sadness in pleading length of sadness and no sorrow. No sorrow and no sadness length of sadness.

A girl addresses a bountiful supply of seed to feed a chicken. Address a bountiful supply of trees to shade them. Address a bountiful supply to them.

A guardian.

In days and nights beside days are followed by daisies. We find them and they find them and water finds them and they grow best where we meant to suggest. We suggested that we would go there again. A woman leaning forward.

She was necessarily taken to be no taller.

A girl.

If she may say what she will say she will say that there were a quantity of voices and they were white and then darker.

A woman with two bundles.

If she did it to be useful if she did not even attract the same throne. What did I say. Did royalists say that they did not have this to say to-day.

Standing.

Measure an alarm by refusing to alarm them and they this not as a disaster but as a pretension. Do you pretend to be unfavourable to their thought.

Eighth.

If you hold heavily heavily instead. Instead of in there. Did you not intend to show this to them.

Saint.

A Saint.

Saint and very well I thank you.

Two in bed.

Two in bed.

Yes two in bed.

They had eaten.

Two in bed.

They had eaten.

Two in bed.

She says weaken

If she said.

She said two in bed.

She said they had eaten.

She said yes two in bed.

She said weaken.

Do not acknowledge to me that seven are said that a Saint and seven that it is said that a saint in seven that there is said to be a saint in seven.

Now as to illuminations.

They are going to illuminate and every one is to put into their windows their most beautiful object and every one will say and the streets will be crowded everyone will say look at it. They do say look at it.

To look at it. They will look at it. They will say look at it.

If it should rain they will all be there. If it should be windy they will all be there. Who will be there. They will all be there.

Names of streets named after the saint. Names of places named after the saint. Names of saints named after the saint. Names of sevens named after the saint. The saints in sevens.

Noon-light for Roman arches.

He left fairly early.

Let them make this seen.

Louise giggled.

Michael was not angry nor was he stuttering nor was he able to silence them. He was angry he was stuttering and he was able to answer them.

They were nervous.

Josephine was able to be stouter. Amelia was really not repaid.

And the taller younger and weaker older and straighter one said come to eat again.

Michael was not able to come angrily to them. He angrily muttered for them.

Louise was separated to Heloise and not by us. So then you see saints for them.

Louise.

Heloise.

Amelia.

Josephine.

Michael and Elinor.

Seven, a saint in seven and in this way it was not Paul. Paul was deprived of nothing. Saint in seven a saint in seven.

Who.

A saint in seven.

Owls and bees.

If you please.

Paul makes honey and orange trees.

Michael makes coal and celery.

Louise makes rugs and reasonably long.

Heloise makes the sea and she settles well away from it.

Amelia does not necessarily please. She does not place herself near linen.

Josephine measures a little toy and she may be no neater.

Eleanor has been more satisfied and feeble. She does not look as able to stay nor does she seem as able to go any way.

Saints in seven makes italics sombre.

I make fun of him of her.

I make fun of them.

They make fun of them of this. They make fun of him of her.

She makes fun of of them of him.

He makes fun of them of her.

They make fun of her.

He makes fun of them.

She makes fun of him.

I make fun of them.

We have made them march. She has made a procession.

A saint in seven and there were six. A saint in seven and there were eight. A saint in seven.

If you know who pleads who precedes who succeeds.

He leads.

He leads and they follow. One two three four and as yet there are no more.

A saint in seven.

And when do they sleep again. A ring around the moon is seen to follow the moon and the moon is in the center of the ring and the ring follows the moon.

Sleeping, to-day sleeping to-day is nearly a necessity and to-day coals reward the five. One two three four five. Corals reward the five. In this way they are not leaning with the intention of being a hindrance to satisfaction.

A saint in seven is told of bliss.

I will know why they open so.

Carefully seen to be safely arranged.

One two three four five six seven. A saint in seven.

To begin in this way.

Carefully attended carefully attended to this.

If we had seen if they had seen if we had seen what was in between, they went very slowly so that we might know but to be slow and we were not slow and to show and they showed it and we did not decide because we had already come to a decision.

Saints in seven are a very large number. Seven and seven

is not as pretty as five and five. And five and five need not mean more. Now to remember how to mean to be gay. Gayly the boxer the boxer very gayly depresses no one. He seems he does seem he dreams he does dream he seems to dream.

Extra readiness to recall himself to these places. Thanks so much for startling. Do not by any means start to worship in order to be excellent. He is excellent again and again.

A saint can share expenses he can share and he can be interested in their place. Their place is plentifully sprinkled as they bend forward. And no one does mean to contend any more.

A saint in seven plentifully.

None of it is good.

It has been said that the woods are the poor man's overcoat but we have found the mountains which are near by and not high can be an overcoat to us. Can he be an overcoat to us.

A saint in seven wished to be convinced by us that the mountains near by and not high can give protection from the wind. One does not have to consider rain because it cannot rain here. A saint in seven wishes to be convinced by us that the mountains which are near by would act as a protection to those who find it cold and yet when one considers that nothing is suffering neither men women children lambs roses and broom, broom is yellow when one considers that neither broom, roses lambs men children and women none of them suffer neither here nor in the mountains near by the mountains are not high and if it were not true that every one had to be sure that that they were there every one would be persuaded that they had persuaded that they had been persuaded that this was true.

He told us that he knew that the name was the same. A saint in seven can declare this to be true.

He comes again. Yes he comes again and what does he say he says do you know this do you refuse no more than you give. That is the way to spell it do you refuse no more than you give.

He searches for more than one word. He manages to eat finally and as he does so and as he does so and as he does so he manages to cut the water in two. If water is flowing down a canal and it is understood that the canal is full if the canal has many outlets for irrigation purposes and the whole country is irrigated if even the mountains are irrigated by the canal and in this way neither oil nor seeds nor wood is needed and it is needed by them why then do the examples remain here examples of industry of cowardice of pleasure of reasonable sight seeing of objections and of lands and oceans. We do not know oceans. We do not know measures. Measure and measure and then decide that a servant beside, what is a servant beside. No one knows how easily he can authorise him to go, how easily she can authorise her to go how easily they can authorise them to come and to go. I authorise you to come and go. I authorise you to go. I authorise you to go and come.

SITWELL EDITH SITWELL

In a minute when they sit when they sit around her.
Mixed it with to who. One two two one two two. Mixed it
with two who.

Weeks and weeks able and weeks.

No one sees the connection between Lily and Louise, but I do.

After each has had after each has had, after each has had had had had it.

Change in time.

A change in time is this, if a change in time. If a change in time is this. If a change in time.

Did she come to say who.

Not to remember weeks to say and asking, not to remember weeks to-day. Not to remember weeks to say. Not to remember weeks to say and asking.

And now a bow.

When to look when to look up and around when to look down and around when to look down and around when to look around and around and altered.

Just as long as any song.

And now altogether different.

It was in place of places and and it was here.

Supposing she had had a key supposing she had answered, supposing she had had to have a ball supposing she had it fall and she had answered. Supposing she had it and in please, please never see so.

As much even as that, even can be added to by in addition, listen.

Table table to be table to see table to be to see to me, table to me table to be table to table to table to it. Exactly as they did it when when she was not and not and not so. After that perhaps.

She had a way of she had a way of not the name.

Little reaching it away.

As afternoon to borrow.
It made a difference.
This is most.
Introduces.
This is for her and not for Mabel Weeks.
She could not keep it out.
Introduces have and heard.
Miss Edith Sitwell have and heard.
Introduces have and had.
Miss Edith Sitwell have and had.
Introduces have and had introduces have and had and heard.
Miss Edith Sitwell have and had and heard.
Left and right.
Part two of Part one.
If she had a ball at all, if she had a ball at all too.
Fill my eyes no no.
It was and held it.
The size of my eyes.
Why does one want to or to and to, when does one want to
and to went to.
To know it as well as all there.
If a little other more not so little as before, now they knew
and that and so.
What in execute.
Night is different from bright.
When he was a little sweeter was he.
Part two.
There was a part one.
He did seem a little so.
Half of to mention it at all.

And now to allow literally if and it will if and it does if and it has if and it is.

Never as much as a way.

How does she know it.

She could be as she sleeps and as she wakes all day. She could be as she sleeps and as she wakes all day is it not so.

It leads it off of that.

Please carried at.

Twice at once and carry.

She does and care to and cover and never believe in an and being narrow.

Happily say so.

What is as added.

And opposite.

Now it has to be something entirely different and it is.

Not turned around.

No one knows two two more.

Lose and share all and more.

Very easily ariscs.

It very easily arises.

Absently faces and by and by we agree.

By and by faces apparently we agree.

Apparently faces by and by we agree.

By and by faces apparently we agree.

Apparently faces by and by we agree.

JEAN COCTEAU

NEEDS be needs be needs be near.
Needs be needs be needs be.

This is where they have their land astray.
        Two say.
This is where they have their land astray
Two say.
Needs be needs be needs be
Needs be needs be needs be near.
        Second time.
It may be nearer than two say.
Near be near be near be
Needs be needs be needs be
Needs be needs be needs be near.
He was a little while away.
Needs be nearer than two say.
Needs be needs be needs be needs be.
Needs be needs be needs be near.
He was away a little while.
        And two say.
He was away a little while
He was away a little while
        And two say.

        Part two.

Part two and part one
Part two and part two
Part two and part two
Part two and part one.
He was near to where they have their land astray.
He was near to where they have two say.
Part two and near one. Part one and near one.
Part two and two say.
Part one and part two and two say.

54

He was as when they had nearly their declamation their declaration their verification their amplification their rectification their elevation their safety their share and there where. This is where they have the land astray. Two say.

Put it there in there there where they have it. Put it there in there there where they halve it.

Put it there in there there and they have it. Put it there in there there and they halve it.

He nearly as they see the land astray.

By that and in that and mine.

He nearly as they see he nearly as they see the land he nearly as they see the land astray.

And by that by that time mine. He nearly as they see the land astray by that by that time by that time by that time mine by that time mine by that time. By that time and mine and by that time and mine.

He nearly when they see the land astray.

By that time and mine.

Not nearly apart.

Part and not partly and not apart and not nearly not apart.

When he when he was is and does, when he partly when he partly when he is and was and partly when he and partly when he does and was and is and partly and apart and when he and apart and when he does and was and when he is.

When he is partly
When he is apart.
Particularly for him
He makes it be the rest of the day for them as well.
Partly partly begun
The rest and one
One part partly begun.

Partly begun one and one.

One and one and partly begun and one and one partly begun. Partly begun part partly begun part partly begun and one and part and one and partly begun and part partly begun.

Partly begun.

Did they need the land astray.

Partly begun and one.

Did they need the land astray and partly begun and one.

Did they need it to be the rest of the day did they need it to be the land astray partly begun and one part partly begun part part partly begun part partly begun and one.

They need it as they had it for themselves to be the rest and next to that and by this who were as it must for them.

He knew and this.

When half is May how much is May.

Whole and here there and clear shall and dear well and well at that. Well is a place from which water is drawn and what is drawn.

A well is a place from which out of which water is drawn and what is drawn.

A well is a place out of which water is drawn and water is drawn. A well is a place out of which water is drawn and what is drawn.

A well is a place out of which water is drawn.

A well is a place from which water is drawn.

They made it that they could be where they were.

Where they were when they were where they were.

He had it as is his in his hand.

Hand and head.

Head and hand and land

two say

as

ours.

They make them they make them they make them they make them they make them they make them at once.

And nearly when he knows.

As long as head as short as said as short as said as long as head.

And this as long and this as long and this and this and so who makes the wedding go and so and so.

It is usually not my habit to mention anything but now having the habit of addressing I am mentioning it as anything.

Having the habit of addressing having the habit of expressing having the habit of expressing having the habit of addressing.

A little away

And a little away.

Everything away.

Everything away.

Everything and away.

Everything and away.

Away everything away.

It is very extraordinary that it is just as interesting.

When it was it was it was there

There there.

Eight eight and eight, eight eight and eight. Eight eight and eight and and eight.

After all seeing it with that and with that never having heard a third a third too, too.

When there a there and where is where and mine is mine and in is in who needs a shred.

They needed three when this you see when this you see and three and three and it was two more they must.

They must address with tenderness

Two him.

G. STEIN

It was not always finished for this once.

Once or twice and for this then they had that and as well as having it so that and this and all and now and believe for it all when they and shall and when and for and most and by and with and this and there and as and by and will and when and can and this and this and than and there and find and there and all and with and will it and with it and with it and they and this and there and so and I and in and all and all and if and if and if and if and if and if now. Now need never alter anyhow.

Anyhow means furls furls with a chance chance with a change change with as strong strong with as will will with as sign sign with as west west with as most most with as in in with as by by with as change change with as reason reason to be lest lest they did when when they did for for they did there and then. Then does not celebrate the there and then.

Who knows it.

I wish to be very well pleased and I thank you.

GERTRUDE STEIN.

AN AMERICAN AND FRANCE

AN AMERICAN AND FRANCE

AMERICA is my country and Paris is my home town and it is as it has come to be.

After all anybody is as their land and air is. Anybody is as the sky is low or high, the air heavy or clear and anybody is as there is wind or no wind there. It is that which makes them and the arts they make and and the work they do and the way they eat and the way they drink and the way they learn and everything.

And so I am an American and I have lived half my life in Paris, not the half that made me but the half in which I made what I made.

And why is Paris my home town, because after all that is just what it is, it is my home town.

It is very natural that every one who makes anything inside themselves that is makes it entirely out of what is in them does naturally have to have two civilizations. They have to have the civilization that makes them and the civilization that has nothing to do with them.

What is adventure and what is romance. Adventure is making the distant approach nearer but romance is having what is where it is which is not where you are stay where it is. So those who create things do not need adventure but they do need romance they need that something that is not for them stays where it is and that they can know that it is there where it is.

It has always been true of all who make what they make come out of what is in them and have nothing to do with what is necessarily existing outside of them it is inevitable that they have always wanted two civilizations. The Renaissance needed the greeks, as the modern painter needed the negroes as the English writers have needed Italy and as many Americans have needed Spain or France. There is no possibility of mixing up the other civilization with yourself you are you and if you are you in your own civilization you are apt to mix yourself up too much with your civilization but when it is another civilization a complete other a romantic other another that stays there where it is you in it have freedom inside yourself which if you are to do what is inside yourself and nothing else is a very useful thing to have happen to you and so America is my country and Paris is my home town.

What is that romantic thing that does happen to you.

It begins it practically always begins as soon as the civilization that is you comes to be you that is as soon as you know anything.

What is the difference between romantic and historical. That is very important because that determines which civilization which second civilization you will need in your business in your business as a creator.

Historical is different from romantic and to us Americans England is historical while France and Spain are romantic.

The other day we were talking about a rather strange thing that so many Spanish painters married Russians and wondered why and that the Russian marriages well do not turn out well. A Russian explained. She said you see she said Russians and Spaniards have many superficial things in common and so they come together, but as soon as they are together they know that those superficial things carry them just far enough to know that they have nothing at all in common and so there is disaster.

All this has a great deal to do with romance and with history nothing whatever to do with adventure but as I say adventure has really nothing to do with creation, because the distant thing being brought nearer ceases to have any existence inside in one and therefore adventure has no relation to creation. Any one can realise that.

But romance and history, where are we when there is that. There always is romance and there always is history, and it seems as if the two are alike but they are not certainly not necessarily that.

Romance is the outside thing, that remains the outside thing and remaining there has its own existing and so although it is outside it is inside because it being outside and staying outside it is always a thing to be felt inside. Now history is different. History can be outside but as outside it continues and as it continues it cannot remain inside you and so in this way it is very different from romance. Romance is there but it does not continue it has no time it is neither past nor present nor future it is there because it is something with which you cannot come into contact as it exists of itself and by itself and looks as it does where it is.

To an American England can of course be romantic, it very often is, but it is historical it completely is and therefore like the Spaniard and the Russian even though eventually the American and Englishman find that they are different they can to a certain extent progress together and so they can have a time sense together they can have a past present and future together and so they are more history than romance and so living in England does not free the American the way living in France frees him because the french and the American do not have the sense of going on together, from the beginning they know that there is no going on together no past present and future and so it is there existing outside one from the other and if a thing exists completely outside then there is no doubt that there is no past present and future, and there is nothing that any one creating anything needs more than that there is no time sense inside in them no past present or future.

So let me tell the difference between France and England in the inside life of an American.

There is another matter that must be settled before we can find out what is the second civilization needed by anyone who is to be a creator. And that is the size of the world. That is going to be a very serious matter. The size of the world getting inevitably getting smaller and smaller and less and less different is going to be a very serious matter.

In the early civilizations when any one was to be a creator a writer or a painter and he belonged to his own civilization and could not know another, he inevitably in order to know another had made for him it was one of the things that inevitably existed a language which as an ordinary member of his civilization did not exist for him. That is really really truly the reason why they always had a special language to write which was not the language that was spoken, now it is generally considered that this was because of the necessity of religion and mystery but actually the writer could not write unless he had the two civilizations coming together the one he was and the other that was there outside him and creation is the opposition of one of them to the other. This is very interesting. Really this is very true, the written thing is not the spoken thing and the written thing exists there because the writing that is in the old civilization was a something with which there was not really anything existing because it existed there and it remained there and the one writing connected that with himself only by creating. That is what romance is and is not what history is. History is what has happened and so having happened it is something that might happen and so does not exist for and by itself and is therefore not romantic.

This is all really very exciting, and you see the trouble is that now the world is very small, history that is anything happening goes on, and the difference between writing and speaking is nothing well then where are we, where are we to find two civilizations which I insist any one creating anything needs to have if he is to create anything.

Everybody more or less knows that this is a trouble now, they try everything but every one more or less knows that this is a trouble now.

When I began being well of course everything is always a trouble, that is what everything is but nevertheless finding the other civilization was not so much of a bother as it is now, the world was not yet as small as it has become not yet.

When a thing is completely different then it is not romantic then it comes nearer to being an adventure, the Orient to the Occident has to be that, but to an American particularly a Pacific Coast American the Orient was not a romance not necessarily an adventure, it was something different altogether, it really was not there and so it did not matter in spite of the fact that if it were there there would be no difficulty in knowing all about its being there and so once more it did not matter. It was therefore neither romance nor history and so it was not the second civilization. Have I made myself clear. At any rate it was neither romance nor history and it did not matter. Now the world has become small and once more completely the Orient has come to be here, not there but here and once more as a second civilization it does not exist and so it does not matter.

There are so many things to say besides about the part in between between the Orient and the Occident and these might come to matter, indeed they are the romance to lots of you who are here now, and so have the world not to be too small so that any one who is to create can have his two civilizations which are necessary.

But to tell what France meant to me and why Paris became my home town. That is what I wish now a very little to do.

Any one can remember what they saw but not nearly enough to tell. But any one can remember what there was well really well enough to tell.

They are two things you live in what you do and what you have. Mostly if you are going to be any one who is going to do anything dependent entirely upon what is within what you have is mostly what you read. What you do is what you do there is nothing more to be said about that. But what you have in other words what you read there is a great deal to be said about that.

What I read was all English some American but mostly all English and so what I had was English and was that that I had romantic. More historical than romantic it all really had happened. I could not have it so much if at all really had not happened and it had happened and it was happening. But then there were french things and some Spanish. To be sure I read them in English but they were romantic they had not happened. Cinq Mars, deVigny, Dumas, Don Quixote, Jules Verne, Georges Sand they were there but they had not happened not like the Stuarts and Walter Scott happened no not at all. That was what made them romantic that they were there but they had not happened. Shakespeare had happened, Pilgrim's Progress had happened, the Arabian Nights had happened but the french and Spanish things had not happened they were there but they had not happened and so they were to me romantic but not historical, they were there for me but I did not live in them not as I did in the English books where the things had happened. There are a lot of young Americans today for whom Proust does that, it is there but it has not happened and so as deVigny and Georges Sand and Balzac and Jules Verne were romantic to me so Proust is to them. They do not live in it as they do in the English thing but it is there and it has not happened.

As I say the Arabian Nights the Oriental thing is a different thing, it can be far enough away so its happening is not an important thing, but the french and Spanish thing to the American has that about it, it is there it is near but it has not happened.

And so Americans go to Paris and they are free not to be connected with anything happening.

That is what foreignness is, that it is there but it does not happen. England to an American English writing to an American is not in this sense a foreign thing. And so we go to Paris. That is a great many of us go to Paris.

And when we live in Paris what is it that it is.

But there is another thing that happened before going to Paris and that is pictures. Of course lots of people have painted pictures but they were old pictures, in the nineteenth century the only pictures that were pictures were french pictures and that began as soon as one began.

I was about only ten years old when I saw the Man with the Hoe by Millet and that was a natural thing and a completely foreign thing because the fields were french fields and the hoe was a french hoe and the man was a french man and yet it was really the fields hoes and men and all three together. It is very important to every one that all the nineteenth cen-

68

tury painting was french painting, there is no doubt about it nineteenth century painting was french painting and I like to look at painting. One did of course when one was brought up in California see Japanese prints and American etchings but the only nineteenth century painting was french painting, and so to me Paris was a natural thing.

Just as one needs two civilizations so one needs two occupations the thing one does and the thing that has nothing to do with what one does. Writing and reading is to me synonymous with existing, but painting well looking at paintings is something that can occupy me and so relieve me from being existing. And anybody has to have that happen.

And now why is french painting the only nineteenth century painting I am sure I do not know but it is. The twentieth century tends to be Spanish but Spain in France, but Spanish never the less, but the nineteenth century painting was all french. And I suppose that has a great deal to do with something. Why is all the nineteenth century painting french. It is there is practically no other and it is practically the only century of which that is true. The whole nineteenth century was created as painting by France and I wonder why but anyway it is. There is no getting away from it. At the end of the century it became Spanish and just now well just now we cannot worry about it.

And because France did produce all the painting that the nineteenth century produced those of us who had nothing to do with painting except to look at it lived in France.

And that was natural enough because wherever it is as it is is the place where those who have to be left alone have to be.

Whether France or Paris left you alone because it was the place where all the nineteenth century painting was being made or all the nineteenth century painting was being made there because they let you alone I do not know but it is all so.

France was friendly and it let you alone, and so there it was and there you were, since the war perhaps not so much and so painting has become Spanish, it was becoming so just at the end.

To be friendly and to let you alone, to be there and to be not needed by it, that was France in the nineteenth century and so everybody was there and everybody and anybody did what they did in it not being of it because one could not be of it since it was there. How can you be of anything if it is there of course not. Anybody can realize that.

Very well that was nineteenth century that is pre-war Paris and I lived there and then there was the war and then after the war I lived there. As I said America is my country and Paris is my home town.

It is not what France gave you but what it did not take away from you that was important.

After all it is that that is important. After all what you are you are even if you are not all of it, but any one being interested in you you are likely to lose it and that is what France did it was not interested in you. That is really what Paris did. Alas the after-war has made France interested in you, perhaps really interested in you well we will see but to us who know France the France that took nothing from you because it was there and had no need of you not of you but of what anything meant in being you that France took nothing from you and so it was where those doing anything from all that was inside them needed to be living. And it was what we did, it was what I did and this is all that I can say about this thing. 1936

BASKET

IDENTITY A POEM

Play 1

I AM I because my little dog knows me. The figure wanders on alone.

71

The little dog does not appear because if it did then there would be nothing to fear.

It is not known that anybody who is anybody is not alone and if alone then how can the dog be there and if the little dog is not there is it alone. The little dog is not alone because no little dog could be alone. If it were alone it would not be there.

So then the play has to be like this.

The person and the dog are there and the dog is there and the person is there and where oh where is their identity, is the identity there anywhere.

I say two dogs but say a dog and a dog.

The human mind.	The human mind does play.
The human mind.	Plays because it plays.
Human Nature.	Does not play because it does not play again.

It might desire something but it does not play again.

And so to make excitement and not nervousness into a play.

And then to make a play with just the human mind.

Let us try.

To make a play with human nature and not anything of the human mind.

Pivoines smell like magnolias

Dogs smell like dogs

Men smell like men

And gardens smell differently at different seasons of the year.

Play 2

Try a play again
Every little play helps
Another play.

There is any difference between resting and waiting.
Does a little dog rest.
Does a little dog wait.
What does the human mind do.
What does human nature do.

A play.

There is no in between in a play.
A play could just as well only mean two.
Then it could do
It could really have to do.
The dog.   What could it do.
The human mind.   The human mind too
Human nature.   Human nature does not have it to do.
  What can a dog do and with waiting too.
  Yes there is when you have not been told when to cry.
  Nobody knows what the human mind is when they are drunk.
  Everybody who has a grandfather has had a great grandfather and that great grandfather has had a father. This actually is true of a grandmother who was a granddaughter and grandfather had a father.
  Any dog too.
  Any time anyone who knows how to write can write to any brother.
  Not a dog too.
  A dog does not write too.

Another Play.

But. But is a place where they can cease to distress her.

Another Play.

It does not make any difference what happens to anybody if it does not make a difference what happens to them.

This no dog can say.

Not any dog can say not ever when he is at play.

And so dogs and human nature have no identity.

It is extraordinary that when you are acquainted with a whole family you can forget about them.

Another Play.

A man coming.

Yes there is a great deal of use in a man coming but will he come at all if he does come will he come here.

How do you like it if he comes and looks like that. Not at all later. Well any way he does come and if he likes it he will come again.

Later when another man comes

He does not come.

Girls coming. There is no use in girls coming.

Well any way he does come and if he likes it he will come again.

Part IV

The question of identity.

A play.

I am I because my little dog knows me.

Which is he.

No which is he.

Say it with tears, no which is he.

I am I why.

So there.

I am I where.

74

Act I Scene III

I am I because my little dog knows me.

Act I Scene

Now this is the way I had played that play.
But not at all not as one is one.

Act I Scene I

Which one is there I am I or another one.
Who is one and one or one is one.
I like a play of acting so and so and a dog my dog is any one
of not one.
But we in America are not displaced by a dog oh no no
not at all not at all at all displaced by a dog.

Scene I

A dog chokes over a ball because it is a ball that choked
any one.

Part I Scene I

He has forgotten that he has been choked by a ball no not
forgotten because this one the same one is not the one that
can choke any one.

Scene I Act I

I am I because my little dog knows me, but perhaps he does
not and if he did I would not be I. Oh no oh no.

Act I Scene I

When a dog is young he seems to be a very intelligent one.
But later well later the dog is older.
And so the dog roams around he knows the one he knows
but does that make any difference.

A play is exactly like that.
Chorus   There is no left of right without remembering.
And remembering.
They say there is no left and right without remembering.
Chorus   But there is no remembering the human mind.
Tears   There is no chorus in the human mind.
The land is flat from on high and when they wander.
Chorus   Nobody who has a dog forgets him. They may
              leave him behind. Oh yes they may leave him
              behind.
Chorus   There is no memory in the human mind.
And the result
May be and the result
If I am I then my little dog knows me.
The dog listens while they prepare food.
Food might be connected by the human mind but it is not.

Scene II

And how do you like what you are
And how are you what you are
And has this to do with the human mind.
Chorus   And has this to do with the human mind.
Chorus   And is human nature not at all interesting.
              It is not.

Scene II

I am I because my little dog knows me.
Chorus   That does not prove anything about you it only
              proves something about the dog.
Chorus   Of course nobody can be interested in human
              nature.
Chorus   Nobody is.

Chorus	Nobody is interested in human nature.
Chorus	Not even a dog
Chorus	It has nothing to do human nature has nothing to do with anything.
Chorus	No not with a dog
Tears	No not with a dog.
Chorus	I am I because my little dog knows
Chorus	Yes there I told you human nature is not at all interesting.

Scene III

And the human mind.

Chorus	And the human mind
Tears	And the human mind
Chorus	Yes and the human mind.

Of course the human mind

Has that anything to do with I am I because my little dog knows me.

What is the chorus.

Chorus	What is the chorus.

Anyway there is the question of identity.

What is the use of being a little boy if you are to grow up to be a man.

Chorus	No the dog is not the chorus.

Scene II

Any scene may be scene II

Chorus	And act II

No any act can be act one and two.

Scene II

I am I because my little dog knows me even if the little

77

dog is a big one and yet a little dog knowing me does not really make me be I no not really because after all being I I am I has really nothing to do with the little dog knowing me, he is my audience, but an audience never does prove to you that you are you.

And does a little dog making a noise make the same noise.

He can almost say the b in bow wow.

I have not been mistaken.

Chorus   Some kinds of things not and some kinds of things.

Scene I

I am I yes sir I am I.

I am I yes madame am I I.

When I am I am I I.

And my little dog is not the same thing as I am I.

Chorus   Oh is it.

With tears in my eyes oh is it.

And there we have the whole thing

Am I I.

And if I am I because my little dog knows me am I I.

Yes sir am I I.

The dog answers without asking because the dog is the answer to anything that is that dog.

But not I.

Without tears but not I.

Act I Scene I

The necessity of ending is not the necessity of beginning.

Chorus   How finely that is said.

78

Scene II

An end of a play is not the end of a day.

Scene IV

After giving.

WHAT ARE MASTER-PIECES AND WHY ARE THERE SO FEW OF THEM

WHAT ARE MASTER-PIECES AND WHY ARE THERE SO FEW OF THEM

I was almost going to talk this lecture and not write and read it because all the lectures that I have written and read in America have been printed and although possibly for you they might even being read be as if they had not been printed still there is something about what has been written having been printed which makes it no longer the property of the one who wrote it and therefore there is no more reason why the writer should say it out loud than anybody else and therefore one does not.

Therefore I was going to talk to you but actually it is impossible to talk about master-pieces and what they are because talking essentially has nothing to do with creation. I talk a lot I like to talk and I talk even more than that I may say I talk most of the time and I listen a fair amount too and as I have said the essence of being a genius is to be able to talk and listen to listen while talking and talk while listening but and this is very important very important indeed talking has nothing to do with creation. What are master-pieces and why after all are there so few of them. You may say after all there are a good many of them but in any kind of proportion with everything that anybody who does anything is doing there are really very few of them. All this summer I meditated and wrote about this subject and it finally came to be a discussion of the relation of human nature and the human mind and identity. The thing one gradually comes to find out is that one has no identity that is when one is in the act of doing anything. Identity is recognition, you know who you are because you and others remember anything about yourself but essentially you are not that when you are doing anything. I am I because my little dog knows me but, creatively speaking the little dog knowing that you are you and your recognising that he knows, that is what destroys creation. That is what makes school. Picasso once remarked I do not care who it is that has or does influence me as long as it is not myself.

It is very difficult so difficult that it always has been difficult but even more difficult now to know what is the relation of human nature to the human mind because one has to know what is the relation of the act of creation to the subject the creator uses to create that thing. There is a great deal of nonsense talked about the subject of anything. After all there is always the same subject there are the things you see and there are human beings and animal beings and everybody you might say since the beginning of time knows practically commencing at the beginning and going to the end everything about these things. After all any woman in any village or men either if you like or even children know as much of human psychology as any writer that ever lived. After all there are things you do know each one in his or her way knows all of them and it is not this knowledge that makes master-pieces. Not at all not at all at all. Those who recognise master-pieces say that is the reason but it is not. It is not the way Hamlet reacts to his father's ghost that makes the master-piece, he might have reacted according to Shakespeare in a dozen other ways and everybody would have been as much impressed by the psychology of it. But there is no psychology in it, that is not probably the way any young man would react to the ghost of his father and there is no particular reason why they should. If it were the way a young man could react to the ghost of his father then that would be something anybody in any village would know they could talk about it talk about it endlessly but that would not make a master-piece and that brings us once more back to the subject of identity. At any moment when you are you you are you without the memory of yourself because if you remember yourself while you are you you are not for purposes of creating you. This is so important because it has so much to do with the question of a writer to his audience. One of the things that I discovered in lecturing was that gradually one ceased to hear what one said one heard what the audience hears one say, that is the reason that oratory is practically never a master-piece very rarely and very rarely history, because history deals with people who are orators who hear not what they are not what they say but what their audience hears them say. It is very interesting that letter writing has the same difficulty, the letter writes what the other person is to hear and so entity does not exist there are two present instead of one and so once again creation breaks down. I once wrote in writing *The Making of Americans* I write for myself and strangers but that was merely a literary formalism for if I did write for myself and strangers if I did I would not really be writing because already then identity would take the place of entity. It is awfully difficult, action is direct and effective but after all action is necessary and anything that is necessary has to do with human nature and not with the human mind. Therefore a master-piece has esssentially not to be necessary, it has to be that is it has to exist but it does not have to be necessary it is not in response to necessity as action is because the minute it is necessary it has in it no possibility of going on.

To come back to what a master-piece has as its subject. In writing about painting I said that a picture exists for and in itself and the painter has to use objects landscapes and people as a way the only way that he is able to get the picture to exist. That is every one's trouble and particularly the trouble just now when every one who writes or paints has gotten to be

86

abnormally conscious of the things he uses that is the events the people the objects and the landscapes and fundamentally the minute one is conscious deeply conscious of these things as a subject the interest in them does not exist.

You can tell that so well in the difficulty of writing novels or poetry these days. The tradition has always been that you may more or less describe the things that happen you imagine them of course but you more or less describe the things that happen but nowadays everybody all day long knows what is happening and so what is happening is not really interesting, one knows it by radios cinemas newspapers biographies autobiographies until what is happening does not really thrill any one, it excites them a little but it does not really thrill them. The painter can no longer say that what he does is as the world looks to him because he cannot look at the world any more, it has been photographed too much and he has to say that he does something else. In former times a painter said he painted what he saw of course he didn't but anyway he could say it, now he does not want to say it because seeing it is not interesting. This has something to do with master-pieces and why there are so few of them but not everything.

So you see why talking has nothing to do with creation, talking is really human nature as it is and human nature has nothing to do with master-pieces. It is very curious but the detective story which is you might say the only really modern novel form that has come into existence gets rid of human nature by having the man dead to begin with the hero is dead to begin with and so you have so to speak got rid of the event before the book begins. There is another very curious thing about detective stories. In real life people are interested in the crime more than they are in detection, it is the crime that is the thing the shock the thrill the horror but in the story it is the detection that holds the interest and that is natural enough because the necessity as far as action is concerned is the dead man, it is another function that has very little to do with human nature that makes the detection interesting. And so always it is true that the master-piece has nothing to do with human nature or with identity, it has to do with the human mind and the entity that is with a thing in itself and not in relation. The moment it is in relation it is common knowledge and anybody can feel and know it and it is not a master-piece. At the same time every one in a curious way sooner or later does feel the reality of a master-piece. The thing in itself of which the human nature is only its clothing does hold the attention. I have meditated a great deal about that. Another curious thing about master-pieces is, nobody when it is created there is in the thing that we call the human mind something that makes it hold itself just the same. The manner and habits of Bible times or Greek or Chinese have nothing to do with ours today but the master-pieces exist just the same and they do not exist because of their identity, that is what any one remembering then remembered then, they do not exist by human nature because everybody always knows everything there is to know about human nature, they exist because they came to be as something that is an end in itself and in that respect it is opposed to the business of living which is relation and necessity. That is what a master-piece is not although it may easily be what a master-piece talks about. It is another one of the curious difficulties a master-piece has that is to begin and end, because actually a master-piece does not do that it does not begin and end if it did it would be of necessity and in relation and that is just what a master-piece is not. Everybody worries about that just now everybody that is what makes them talk about abstract and worry about punctuation and capitals and small letters and what a history is. Everybody worries about that not because everybody knows what a master-piece is but because a certain number have found out what a master-piece is not. Even the very master-pieces have always been very bothered about beginning and ending because essentially that is what a master-piece is not. And yet after all like the subject of human nature master-pieces have to use beginning and ending to become existing. Well anyway anybody who is trying to do anything today is desperately not having a beginning and an ending but nevertheless in some way one does have to stop. I stop.

I do not know whether I have made any of this very clear, it is clear, but unfortunately I have written it all down all summer and in spite of everything I am now remembering and when you remember it is never clear. This is what makes secondary writing, it is remembering, it is very curious you begin to write something and suddenly you remember something and if you continue to remember your writing gets very confused. If you do not remember while you are writing, it may seem confused to others but actually it is clear and eventually that clarity will be clear, that is what a master-piece is, but if you remember while you are writing it will seem clear at the time to any one but the clarity will go out of it that is what a master-piece is not.

All this sounds awfully complicated but it is not complicated at all, it is just what happens. Any of you when you write you try to remember what you are about to write and you will see immediately how lifeless the writing becomes that is why expository writing is so dull because it is all remembered, that is why illustration is so dull because you remember what somebody looked like and you make your illustration look like it. The minute your memory functions while you are doing anything it may be very popular but actually it is dull. And that is what a master-piece is not, it may be unwelcome but it is never dull.

And so then why are there so few of them. There are so few of them because mostly people live in identity and memory that is when they think. They know they are they because their little dog knows them, and so they are not an entity but an identity. And being so memory is necessary to make them exist and so they cannot create master-pieces. It has been said of geniuses that they are eternally young. I once said what is the use of being a boy if you are going to grow up to be a man, the boy and the man have nothing to do with each other, except in respect to memory and identity, and if they have anything to do with each other in respect to memory and identity then they will never produce a master-piece. Do you do you understand well it really does not make much difference because after all master-pieces are what they are and the reason why is that there are very few of them. The reason why is any of you try it just not to be you are you because your little dog knows you. The second you are you because your little dog knows you you cannot make a master-piece and that is all of that.

It is not extremely difficult not to have identity but it is extremely difficult the knowing not having identity. One might say it is impossible but that it is not impossible is proved by the existence of master-pieces which are just that. They are knowing that there is no identity and producing while identity is not.

That is what a master-piece is.

And so we do know what a master-piece is and we also know why there are so few of them. Everything is against them. Everything that makes life go on makes identity and everything that makes identity is of necessity a necessity. And the pleasures of life as well as the necessities help the necessity of identity. The pleasures that are soothing all have to do with identity and the pleasures that are exciting all have to do with identity and moreover there is all the pride and vanity which play about master-pieces as well as about every one and these too all have to do with identity, and so naturally it is natural that there is more identity that one knows about than anything else one knows about and the worst of all is that the only thing that any one thinks about is identity and thinking is something that does so nearly need to be memory and if it is then of course it has nothing to do with a master-piece.

But what can a master-piece be about mostly it is about identity and all it does and in being so it must not have any. I was just thinking about anything and in thinking about anything I saw something. In seeing that thing shall we see it without it turning into identity, the moment is not a moment and the sight is not the thing seen and yet it is. Moments are not important because of course master-pieces have no more time than they have identity although time like identity is what they concern themselves about of course that is what they do concern themselves about.

Once when one has said what one says it is not true or too

true. That is what is the trouble with time. That is what makes what women say truer than what men say. That is undoubtedly what is the trouble with time and always in its relation to master-pieces. I once said that nothing could bother me more than the way a thing goes dead once it has been said. And if it does it it is because of there being this trouble about time.

Time is very important in connection with master-pieces, of course it makes identity time does make identity and identity does stop the creation of master-pieces. But time does something by itself to interfere with the creation of master-pieces as well as being part of what makes identity. If you do not keep remembering yourself you have no identity and if you have no time you do not keep remembering yourself and as you remember yourself you do not create anybody can and does know that.

Think about how you create if you do create you do not remember yourself as you do create. And yet time and identity is what you tell about as you create only while you create they do not exist. That is really what it is.

And do you create yes if you exist but time and identity do not exist. We live in time and identity but as we are we do not know time and identity everybody knows that quite simply. It is so simple that anybody does know that. But to know what one knows is frightening to live what one lives is soothing and though everybody likes to be frightened what they really have to have is soothing and so the master-pieces are so few not that the master-pieces themselves are frightening no of course not because if the creator of the master-piece is frightened then he does not exist without the memory of time and identity, and insofar as he is that then he is frightened and insofar as he is frightened the master-piece does not exist, it looks like it and it feels like it, but the memory of the fright destroys it as a master-piece. Robinson Crusoe and the foot-step of the man Friday is one of the most perfect examples of the non-existence of time and identity which makes a master-piece. I hope you do see what I mean but any way everybody who knows about Robinson Crusoe and the foot-step of Friday knows that that is true. There is no time and identity in the way it happened and that is why there is no fright.

And so there are very few master-pieces of course there are very few master-pieces because to be able to know that is not to have identity and time but not to mind talking as if there was because it does not interfere with anything and to go on being not as if there were no time and identity but as if there were and at the same time existing without time and identity is so very simple that it is difficult to have many who are that. And of course that is what a master-piece is and that is why there are so few of them and anybody really anybody can know that.

What is the use of being a boy if you are going to grow up to be a man. And what is the use there is no use from the standpoint of master-pieces there is no use. Anybody can really know that.

There is really no use in being a boy if you are going to grow up to be a man because then man and boy you can be certain that that is continuing and a master-piece does not continue it is as it is but it does not continue. It is very interesting that no one is content with being a man and boy but he must also be a son and a father and the fact that they all die has some-thing to do with time but it has nothing to do with a master-piece. The word timely as used in our speech is very interesting but you can any one can see that it has nothing to do with master-pieces we all readily know that. The word timely tells that master-pieces have nothing to do with time.

It is very interesting to have it be inside one that never as you know yourself you know yourself without looking and feeling and looking and feeling make it be that you are some one you have seen. If you have seen any one you know them as you see them whether it is yourself or any other one and so the identity consists in recognition and in recognising you lose identity because after all nobody looks as they look like, they do not look like that we all know that of ourselves and of any one. And therefore in every way it is a trouble and so you write anybody does write to confirm what any one is and the more one does the more one looks like what one was and in being so identity is made more so and that identity is not what any one can have as a thing to be but as a thing to see. And it being a thing to see no master-piece can see what it can see if it does then it is timely and as it is timely it is not a master-piece.

There are so many things to say. If there was no identity no one could be governed, but everybody is governed by everybody and that is why they make no master-pieces, and also why governing has nothing to do with master-pieces it has completely to do with identity but it has nothing to do with master-pieces. And that is why governing is occupying but not interesting, governments are occupying but not interesting because master-pieces are exactly what they are not.

There is another thing to say. When you are writing before there is an audience anything written is as important as any other thing and you cherish anything and everything that you have written. After the audience begins, naturally they create something that is they create you, and so not everything is so important, something is more important than another thing, which was not true when you were you that is when you were not you as your little dog knows you.

And so there we are and there is so much to say but anyway I do not say that there is no doubt that master-pieces are master-pieces in that way and there are very few of them.

1936

AFTERWORD

In 1946, the year she died, Gertrude Stein agreed to a transatlantic interview with a friend and admirer, Robert Haas. His questions were put to her on January 5 to 6 at her apartment at 5 rue *Christine in Paris by William S. Sutton, then on military assignment in France. In her replies, Miss Stein made the following observations:*

EVERYTHING I have done has been influenced by Flaubert and Cezanne and this gave me a new feeling about composition. Up to that time composition had consisted of a central idea to which everything else was an accompaniment and separate but was not an end in itself, and Cezanne conceived the idea that in composition one thing was as important as another thing. Each part is as important as the whole and that impressed me enormously and it impressed me so much that I began to write *Three Lives* under this influence and this idea of composition. . . . It was the first time in any language that anyone had used the idea of composition in literature. Henry James had a slight inkling of it and was in some senses a forerunner while in my case I made it stay on the page quite composed. . . . It was not solely the realism of the characters but the realism of the composition which was the important thing, the realism of the composition of my thoughts.

After all to me one human being is as important as another human being and you might say that the landscape has the same values, a blade of grass has the same value as a tree. The realism of the people who did realism before was a realism of trying to make people real. I was not interested in making the people real but in the essence or as the painter would call it value. One cannot live without the other. This was an entirely new idea and had been done a little by the Russians but had not been conceived as a reality until I came along but I got it largely from Cezanne, Flaubert was there as a theme.

In the Making of Americans I began the same thing. In trying to make a history of the world my idea here was to write the life of every individual who could possibly live on the earth. I hoped to realize that ambition. My intention was to cover every possible variety of human type in it. I made endless diagrams of every human being, watching people from windows and so on until I could put down every type of human being that could be on the earth. I wanted each one to have the same value. I was not at all interested in the little or big men but to realize absolutely every variety of human experience that it was possible to have, every type, every style and nuance.

Conception of this has to be based on a real feeling for every human being. The surprises of it are endless. . . . the combination that you don't expect, the relation of men to character you do not expect. It never ends. There are of course people who are more important than others in that they have more importance in the world but this is not essential and it ceases to be. I have no sense of difference in this respect because every human being comprises the combination form. Just as everybody has the vote including women, I think children should, because as a child is conscious of itself then it has to me an existence and has a stake in what happens. Everybody who has that stake has that quality of interest and in the Making of Americans that is what I tried to show.

In writing the Three Lives I was not particularly conscious of the question of style. The style which everybody shouted about surprised me. I was only interested in these other things. In the beginning gradually I became more conscious of it and at that time particularly of a need for evenness. At this time I threw away punctuation. My real objection to it was that it threw away this balance that I was trying to get, this evenness

99

of everybody having the vote and that is the reason I am impatient with punctuation. Finally, I got obsessed with these enormous long sentences and long paragraphs. All that was an effort to get this evenness, and this went on until it sort of exhausted itself.

Then I started to write *Matisse, Picasso and Gertrude Stein.* You will see in each one of these stories that they began in the character of *Making of Americans* and then in about the middle of it words began to be for the first time more important than the sentence structure or the paragraphs. Something happened. I mean I felt a need. I had thought this thing out and felt a need of breaking it down and forcing it into little pieces. I felt that I had lost contact with the words in building up these Beethovian passages [in the *Making of Americans*].

I began to play with words then. Picasso was painting my portrait at that time and he and I used to talk this thing over endlessly. At this time he had just begun on cubism. And I felt that the thing I got from Cezanne was not the last composition. You had to recognize words had lost their value in the nineteenth century particularly towards the end, they had lost much of their variety and I felt that I could not go on, that I had to capture the value of the individual word, find out what it meant and act within it. . . . All through that middle period the interest was with that largely, ending up with *Tender Buttons*. In this I think that there are some of the best uses of words that there are. The movement is simple and holds by little words. I had at the same time a new interest in portraiture. I began then to want to make a more complete picture of each word, and that is when the portrait business started. I wait until each word can intimate some part of each little mannerism. In each one of them I was not satisfied until the whole thing was formed, and it is very difficult to put it down, to explain, in words.

During that middle period I had these two things that were working back to the compositional idea, the idea of portraiture and the idea of the recreation of the word. I took individual words and thought about them until I got their weight and volume complete and put them next to another word and at this same time I found out very soon that there is no such thing as putting them together without sense. It is impossible to put them together without sense. I made innumerable efforts to make words write without sense and found it impossible. Any human being putting down words had to make sense out of them.

All these things interested me very strongly through the middle years from about after the *Making of Americans* until 1911, leading up to *Tender Buttons* which was the apex of that. That was the culmination. Then came the war. . . . As soon as the war was over I settled down and wrote the whole of the *Geography and Plays*. That turned into a very strong interest in play form and then I began to be slowly impressed by the idea of narration.

Human beings are interested in two things. They are interested in the reality and interested in telling about it. I had struggled up to that time with the creation of reality and then I became interested in how you could tell this thing in a way that anybody could understand and at the same time keep true to your values, and the thing bothered me a great deal at that time. I did quite a few plays and portraits and that ended roughly with *Four Saints*, 1932. Most of the things that are in *Useful Knowledge*, including a book of poetry which was not printed, were constant effort and after that I was beginning the narration consisting in plays at first and ending with the *Four Saints*.

After the *Four Saints* the portrait narration began and I went back to the form of narration. At that time I had a certain reputation, no success, but a certain reputation and I was asked to write a biography and I said No. And then as a joke I began to write the *Autobiography of Alice B. Toklas* and at that moment I had made a rather interesting discovery. A young French poet had begun to write and I was asked to translate his poems and there I made a rather startling discovery that other people's words are quite different from one's own and that they cannot be the result of your internal troubles as a writer. They have a totally different sense than when they are your own words. . . . Narrative has a different concept than poetry or even exposition, because you see the narrative in itself is not what is in your mind but what is in somebody else's. And so I did a tour de force with the *Autobiography of Alice B. Toklas* and when I sent the first half to the agent they sent back a telegram to see which one of us had written it. But still I had done what I saw, what you do in translation or in narrative. I had created the point of view of somebody else. Therefore the words ran with a certain smoothness. Shakespeare never expressed any feelings of his own in his sonnets. They have too much smoothness. He did not feel "This is my emotion, I will write it down." If it is your own feeling, one's words have a fullness and violence.

The bulk of my work since then has been largely narration. I think *Paris, France* and *Wars I have Seen* are the most successful. I thought I had done it in *Everybody's Autobiography*. I worked very hard on that and was often very exhausted but it is often confused and not clarified. But in *Wars I have Seen* and in *Paris, France*, to my feeling, I have done it more completely.

I have done the narration because in narration your great problem is the problem of time in telling a story of anybody. And that is why newspaper people never become writers, because they have a false sense of time. . . . You have as a person writing, and all the really great narration has it, you have to denude yourself of time so that writing time does not exist. If time exists your writing is ephemeral. You can have a historical time but for you the time does not exist and if you are writing about the present the time element must cease to exist. I did it unconsciously in the *Autobiography of Alice B. Toklas* but I did it consciously in *Everybody's Autobiography* and in the last thing, *Wars I have Seen*. In it I described something momentous happening under my eyes and I was able to do it without a great sense of time. There should not be a sense of time but an existence suspended in time. That is really where I am at the present moment. I am still largely meditating about this sense of time.

Sinclair Lewis is the perfect example of the false sense of time of the newspaper world. . . . He was always dominated by an artificial time when he wrote *Main Street*. After all, the average human being is selfish and as such is interesting, everybody is and he gives a little character to it. All right, but that is a cliche. He did not create actual human beings at any time. That is what makes it newspaper. Sinclair Lewis is the typical newspaperman and everything he says is newspaper. The difference between a thinker and a newspaperman is that a thinker enters right into things, a newspaperman is superficial.

I write with my eyes not with my ears or mouth. I hate lecturing because you begin to hear yourself talk, because sooner or later you hear your voice and you do not hear what you say. You just hear what they hear you say. As a matter of fact as a writer I write entirely with my eyes. The words as seen by my eyes are the important words and the ears and mouth do not count. I said to Picasso, the other day, "When you were a kid you never looked at things." He seemed to swallow the things he saw but he never looked, and I said, "In recent years you have been looking, you see too much, it is a mistake for you." He said, "You are quite right." A writer should write with his eyes and a painter paint with his ears. You should always paint knowledge which you have acquired not by looking but by swallowing. I have always noticed that in portraits of really great writers the mouth is always firmly closed.

I like a thing simple but it must be simple through complication. Everything must come into your scheme, otherwise you cannot achieve real simplicity. A great deal of this I owe to a great teacher William James. He said, "Never reject anything. Nothing has been proved. If you reject anything, that is the beginning of the end as an intellectual." He was my big influence when I was at college. He was a man who always said "complicate your life as much as you please, it has got to simplify."